CHANGE YOUR LIFE BY LEARNING HOW TO LEARN FASTER

HOW TO CHOOSE WHAT TO LEARN AND LEARN IT FAST.

OLUSEUN WIKIMAN

CHANGE YOUR LIFE BY LEARNING HOW TO LEARN FASTER

OLUSEUN WIKIMAN

SPECIAL THANKS

I thank God for making this book a reality and for wisdom and inspiration. I appreciate my lovely wife and "wikiboy" for their love and support.

Special thanks to all team members and members of Greatlight Visionaries.

Table of contents

THIS BOOK HAS BEEN CALLED THE BOOK OF THE FUTURE.

AN EASY TO READ GUIDE FOR THOSE WHO WANT TO BE

TOMMORROW'S CHAMPIONS.

INTRODUCTION

We are at a knowledge-driven epoch. The more you know the

better your life.

These are unprecedented times. We are in a changing world

where knowledge is surely increasing. It has been said from time

immemorial that we will get to a time when knowledge will be everywhere. It is not a fluke that we have found ourselves in the information age. The curiosity of mankind is infinite; hence, we already had it coming even while the world was going through the Stone Age. Man has always found a way to transfer and hide knowledge.

With the progressive revolutions - the first, second, third, and now the fourth industrial revolution - it became obvious that knowledge will be the order of the day and this has now become a reality to us.

The need for learning also increased with the pandemic. A virus that shut down the world economy and people had to proactively switch over to innovative ways of learning. Aside from the events of death, which is regrettable and sad, it was also unveiled that we are at a knowledge-driven era. The more you know the better your life.

LEARN TO EARN

The way you measure your progress in learning is not about what you remember but what you can apply to create value.

Never think learning does not matter. Knowledge increases asset. Knowledge increases your chances in life. Knowledge makes you relevant and the more you know, the more you become a master. Today's world is "learn to earn." This is a time where your relevance is a function of solutions you provide and problems you solve. You have the ultimate chance to monetize your solutions and earn big. **Therefore, this book is called "the book of the future." It was written with tomorrow in mind.**

Recently, I saw statistics stating that a large percentage of applications in the future will be custom-built. Everyone will want automated processes that particularly and specifically improve their operations and help them maximize profit.

In my daily interaction with people, there now appears to be an overwhelming reality that is dawning on a lot of people. The motivation to learn is now predictably soaring; it is becoming clear we are in a competitive world where even the little things matter a lot. People now realize that if they do not engage themselves in consistent human capacity development, they will become obsolete and unable to fit into a dynamic world.

There is undoubtedly a challenge of information overload, with information overwhelming us. Sometimes, it is like it's a chokehold of the information age, but surviving through this is necessary.

I do not think the solution is to run from knowledge or to deliberately reduce our contact with it. Doing so is exposing ourselves to mediocrity and failure. The solution is to learn how to be fast learners.

'There is nothing that cannot be learned.'

Many great books, models, YouTube videos and academic research publications have been created to help and to encourage people to 'read fast.' However, it should be known that there is a big disparity between reading fast and learning fast. What is the difference between speed reading and speed learning? Which of these is most important? Is it to be a fast reader or to be a fast learner? Reading is important and a large percentage of learning comes from reading. The essence of reading is to acquire knowledge but the essence of learning is to acquire competence. So, read to learn because it is not what you read that will solve problems for you but what you learn. Reading is inevitable for any individual or society that wants to thrive, but the purpose of reading is to learn, and learning is not exclusive to books alone.

The way to measure your progress in learning is not by what you remember but by what you can apply.

Learning can bring opportunities. Opportunities can bring wealth. With learning you create value, you solve problems, you create solutions, you augment services, you make the world a better place.

LIKE MACHINE, LEARNING DEFINE YOUR TARGET

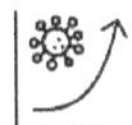

You can learn for any reason but to ensure you are learning at an accelerated rate, define your target.

Many people lose focus because they cannot define what they are learning for and this slows down the learning rate. In Artificial Intelligence (AI), learning rate is optimized to minimize error. Once error is minimized, there is accuracy and accuracy lead to greater intelligence.

Are you learning for leisure or to while away time?

You can learn for any reason but to ensure you are learning at an accelerated rate, define your target.

Defining the target before you embark on any learning endeavor also helps you to select which of the methodologies taught here will work effectively for you. There are different things to learn; it can include languages, art, design, fashion, technology, and other soft skills. Defining the objective will help you select which method works best for different scenarios. It is also important for you to set a goal. Remember the rules of goal setting; SMART - specific, measurable, attainable, realistic and timely and other parameters that define good goal setting. These rules are foundational before you embark on any mission. In artificial intelligence, you have your input data, and you have your target data. The aim is for input to be used to achieve our target. Therefore, throughout the learning cycle, the target calibrates the process and determines how much data is transferred between learning nodes and how accurate the model works. This also works for us even as humans. Without vision, the process perishes.

A friend was invited to train a multinational company on spreadsheet applications. Even though he had basic competency in the use of such application, yet the curriculum he was presented with was at advanced not even intermediate level. This was a mark. He had 2 weeks to prepare went into intensive research. However, his accelerated learning was not a function of the intensity of his research, but a function of his brain capacity increasing and adjusting to take up the challenge of meeting up. Target helps us develop new ideas to do things. Targets helps us find legal shortcuts. Target helps us appreciate routes, templates, tools and again optimizes the brain.

NOT FAST READING BUT FAST LEARNING

To compete in the real world, you transcend from just reading in

volumes to learning in volumes.

This book is NOT about being a fast reader but a fast learner.

There is nothing wrong with speed reading. Both skills are

important in this era. The ability to read fast will help you to

cover large volumes in a shorter time, while the ability to learn fast will help you in acquiring knowledge that can be easily translated to action; hence, improving skills and competence.

Recently, I was talking to a group of young people about why they need to engage in self-education and take advantage of remote learning technologies to increase competence and capacity. Some of them despite knowing the implications of being indifferent to learning, had complaints that due to one thing or the other, they have not been able to complete a book they were reading or complete a course they were studying on digital platforms like Coursera or Udemy. This, however, did not come as a surprise to me. It is obvious some people have low inspiration to learn. Also, society offers a poor incentive to learning and this information age comes with so much information to ingest in so little time. Many of them have not been able to successfully differentiate between the huge information available and the ones that are relevant to them. Being able to judiciously make this distinction is being able to set themselves on a path of fast learning.

Nowadays many social media algorithms, especially the ones which are mandatorily pushed out for commercial reasons, tend to throw many things and everything to us. This itself can be a burden and implies that we as humans also need an algorithm to ensure these algorithms do not overwhelm us with redundancies.

I was talking to a man once who told me he did not think knowledge could solve his problems. He said he had some personality challenges; he lacked frugality and did not know how to concentrate. He said he believed he needed to consult someone in the higher realm of the spirit. **I told him I recognize that sometimes we need spiritual support but several times, lack of knowledge is our greatest hindrance in life.**

As a law student, for example, it becomes mandatory that you read some volume of information as stipulated by your program structure. You cannot skip this part of your education because you are going through a regulated curriculum. Hence, consuming those works of literature, those history books, those books on past judgments, "Lord Denning, Nicholas McBride" and volumes of various other texts become pertinent and inevitable if you must have a law degree.

This also goes for other fields like medicine, social sciences, and even engineering. Throughout your three or four years of stay in college, you are forced and made to read volumes of books. You must read a lot of schoolbooks and pass though compulsory assessments for you to complete your education.

But to compete in the real world. You transcend from just reading in volumes to learning in volumes.

ABOUT LEARNING RATES

Learning rate are tuning parameters that control how much the model can be changed. In response to some mathematical evaluation artificial intelligence, it is significant to study how important it is to tune your learning rates to improve the performance of your model. **Therefore, this implies that accelerating learning will require a change of behavior;** it will require some modification to the way we do things and to the things that we are used to because we want learning to be as accurate as possible. This behavioral pattern will affect the way we think; thus, we will improve our attention span, we will improve our focus, we will reduce distractions, we will form better relationships, we will modify our ego, we will take the necessary sacrifice we require to ensure we optimize our learning potentials.

Accuracy should be seen not just as moving closer to a target but moving away from error till error becomes totally diminished. Hence, our objective here is to take us away from anything that poses erroneous, redundant and a waste of our precious time.

In machine learning, aside from the ability of machines to learn and surf through large data set to find a pattern, they also must increase their learning rate which in their own case is to minimize and maximize a function which they use to provide solutions to real-life problems in real-time.

Time is important. The success and failure of a venture can be dependent on a split second or opportunity.

THE KNOWLEDGE ECONOMY

After you get your degree and you move into the marketplace,

you are now in a knowledge economy.

After you get your degree and you move into the marketplace, you are now in a knowledge economy.

The knowledge economy is the utilization of knowledge to produce goods and services. It refers to a high fraction of skilled workers in the economy of a locality, country or the world, and the idea that most jobs require specialized skills.(Wikipedia)

You will need to demonstrate competence. If you freelance, you will need to show superior skills to rank high in micro job services.

While I was an undergraduate student of engineering, I had one of the best lecturers, professors, doctors, and technologists. They laid a solid foundation for my career in academics and set me up on my path in life. The lessons they taught me and everything I acquired as an engineering student were the bedrock of my research pursuit and I learned lots of things that I remain forever grateful for.

However, as I started my career in the academia and researching institutions and parastatals, I realized that learning is not just about having exposure to books or information.

Learning is not just about buying books or listening to sermons. Learning is not just about what you watch on YouTube or what you read on medium. Learning is more about what you have the competence and have developed capacity in and what you can apply to solve problems and earn a decent living.

I cannot speak for everyone, but I assume the reason why you are reading this book and why you want to learn is that you want to improve an aspect of your life. Either you want to learn how to be a better family man, you want to learn how to control your anger, you want to learn how to cook smoked salmon, or you want to learn how to make money. You want to learn how to invest in stocks or you want to learn how to code, or you want to learn a skill in software development, graphics, video production, digital marketing, creative and critical thinking, partnership, business skills relationship, religion, or politics.

You are looking beyond just reading; you want to understand, you want to improve your learning rate and comprehension.

We are not talking about how to read books faster we are talking about how to learner faster and accelerate comprehension.

The first assignment we will do here is to identify areas where we can acquire knowledge and skills. This will make you aware of your opportunities and open your mind to avenues that may be non-conventional, yet potent enough to help you. You can learn in a classroom or some organized setting. You can learn from reading books. You can learn from accessing audio or videos content. You can learn from a conversation that is either one way or an interaction. You can learn by divine inspiration; you can learn through internship. Sadly, many miss prospects to increase in knowledge because they do not even know where to look for knowledge.

I can go on and on and talk about different avenues you can learn from and in identifying these avenues, we are already on our way to expediting the learning process.

CLEAR THE HIGHWAY

I remember watching a movie were some men were involved in a heist and they needed to fly $10,000,000 to an extremely far and safe location. But the money they were carrying was too heavy. So, they needed to find a way to reduce the weight of what they were carrying because doing so will automatically help them move faster.

Along the way, they had to lose part of the money to ensure they made away successfully with the remaining part due to the limited capacity of the traveling vehicle they were using.

This perhaps can tell us what is happening in our minds when learning. We sometimes tend to suffer exhaustion and tend to slow down because we are carrying so much weight in our minds. If you want to accelerate learning, you need to understand the principle of focus and you need to find a way to increase your mental capacity to learn.

Let me explain another principle in communication engineering. How do we increase the speed of data transmission? It is not just by introducing more communication paths; this can also work but then it will certainly involve more resources. So how do you increase the capacity of your brain? You cannot add another brain to your brain. You cannot increase the size of your head. You cannot expand the size of your brain. Like the movie titled,

"Deep Blue Sea," expanding the size of the brain of a living thing physically might lead to instability in mental activities and results in unintended consequences. So as human beings we need to follow the second method employed in communication, which is reducing noise, **when you reduce the noise in a channel, you have increased the capacity of the channel.** This can be easily explained intuitively. For example, if you are traveling on a road in the peak of the rush hour, no matter how fast your car is, there is a limit at which you can move, but what if you move on that same road at night? I remember one time a friend of mine and I were driving on the Eko bridge in Lagos. We drove on that bridge during rush hour. It took us about 2 hours to get home. Then we drove on the same bridge, the same way, the same distance, the same length, at around 11:30 PM and we got to our destination in under 20 minutes. So how were we able to increase our speed and our capacity? It was simply because we drove at a time when there was less congestion on the road.

DECOMPRESS

But, if you want to be a swift learner, you need to get your mind

ready and maintain the highest form of optimism and

determination

You need to get your mind prepared.

Quell the anxiety and control the excitement.

Learning can be fun and sometimes it can be like walking on a

treadmill...

Usually when you about starting your lessons, it is like walking in

uncharted territory. You can experience nervousness, anxiety, depression, and several emotions. But, if you want to be a swift learner, you need to get your mind ready and maintain the highest form of optimism and determination.

I do not know if this book can help to decongest your mind, but I can tell you that if you want to learn faster, you must learn this principle of decongestion. This same principle is also used in making processors to work more rapidly; what we call increasing THE BUS-WIDTH and introducing a broader bus. By so doing, you introduce more lines for data to travel. Hence, you have quicker movement of data through the microprocessor.

This principle can also be used to help us to increase the rate at which we learn. When there is so much noise and distraction in our minds, it is going to reduce our brain capacity. Therefore, anytime you want to learn, you need to prepare for it. Prepare your mind, prepare your environment, prepare yourself to be able to learn effectively. You can increase your brain capacity by reducing the noise; to concentrate on that thing you are learning. Simply put, mental health is also a factor. Sleep, music, chewing gum are some of the many ways that can help you decompress and keep your brain in a state where the neurons are firing appropriately.

I have heard cases of people who had trauma, experienced the savant syndrome, and become geniuses who had automatic acceleration of brain capacity. But it is said no one really knows how this happens. The good news is that it is also proven from science that when the brain is healthy, it works faster and better. We cannot knock our heads against a brick hoping to kick start this syndrome. That will be a recipe for brain damage. This book is giving us a cocktail that can help us achieve the same result. Remember we have explained that learning has a lot to do with increasing our rate of comprehension and how much we can eventually apply what we are learning. This is an especially important reminder so that we will understand the intent and scope of what this book is about.

FAST LEARNERS FAST EARNERS

A lot of people remain in financial hardship, because of their inability to create value, and you cannot create value without skills and good ideas, and you cannot build skills, without learning and it is learning that helps you to earn.

Do you know that the more you learn, the more you earn, and faster learners are faster earners? People are willing to pay for someone who helps them pass-through difficult problems successfully. There are lots of problems and lots of people ready to exchange money for solutions.

I have encountered countless of this type of situations where people want a solution and they usually do not have the luxury of time. Some people with problems, may not necessarily be operating under a time constraint, BUT you do not have the time even if they gave you enough, because you need to be able to deliver and even exceed their expectations. There is nothing as bad as when opportunity meets non-preparedness.

A lot of people remain in financial hardship, because of their inability to create value, and you cannot create value without skills and good ideas, and you cannot build skills, without learning and it is learning that helps you to earn.

Things will change in the future. People's lifestyles will be augmented, Industries will emerge. Innovation will be a necessity, health, politics, agriculture, and commerce will depend on newer models and logistics for service delivery. We the futuristic thinkers are not trying to overhype the reality. The reality is glaring, and it is coming upon us.

In every field of human life from market to technology to religion and politics, people keep on the lookout for those who can make a contribution and support them meet their objective and meet it suitably. The question now is, are you ready to make yourself available when these opportunities present themselves? Or are you settling for your status quo?

Recently, I was engaged in research. This was when I realized that I do not have the luxury of time. It is not as if time has condensed. No time did not reduce. Human Activity has accelerated immensely and therefore whatever you have to do, do it quicker. Time is moving too fast and it is no different in our daily lives with the surge of human activities and population. Time is getting compressed and therefore, you have to improvise and find ways of catching up when it matters most and making the best of it.

The motivation that you can take advantage of is that fast learners are fast earners. I have met many of them before and I am also one of them.

When we talk about fast learning also be aware, that this also applies to other areas of our social life. Talking about relationships with people, critical thinking, and emotional intelligence. To be successful with human interaction. Learning fast about people's natural character, persona and habits is an asset. And, you do not have all the time to spend with them. Recently my boss commended how fast I adapted to a new system and I found myself. How fast I studied how things work and how fast I learned to adapt to the new environment. This had an impact on my productivity and good service delivery. The Major motivation for me is that I realize enough that swift adaptations have its merits because it makes more people want to work with me and it opens me up to more opportunities to improve and increase competence. This was an incentive for me. Incentives help you to modify your behavior, improve adaptation, and create an avenue for your brain to find all possible away to learn more productively and better.

FUNDAMENTALS

And so, one way to learn quickly is to focus on the fundamentals.

If you miss the fundamentals, you have missed the substance.

Fundamentals are the underlying knowledge which forms a necessary base or core of the central importance to the operation and functioning of anything.

Everything has a fundamental.

Science, physics, accounting, biology, sociology, marketing, thermodynamics etc. Have you heard of the equations that changed the world? Newton law of motion, thermodynamics principles, Faraday's laws, Einstein's equations, Gauss laws etc.

If you never understood these fundamentals, you would spend a long time trying to understand their scope and applications and this will extend your comprehension time.

During my graduate studies, I realized that augmented learning is unavoidable due to the way the world is changing especially. I realized I needed not just to learn, but to learn for capability, because if I do not learn fast, a lot of opportunities will pass me by and some were already passing by. Dan Lok teaches High-income skills. There is no time to wait by and expect society to lower the bar for you with the rate at which new processes, solutions, products, and competitions were occurring around us. So, if we do not learn rapidly, we would be sidelined. If we do not learn swiftly, we will lose a lot of openings.

With an ambition to pursue a doctoral degree, it is imperative that the fundamentals are mastered. You cannot engage in doctoral research without being a keen reader and speedy learner. You have lots of literature to review and need a grip on fundamental concepts. The aim is to contribute to knowledge.

So, a bigger concern is not just being about a fast or vast reader; it means I must lay hold on the ideas. I cannot contribute to what I do not understand; I must understand the keys; I must know how things work as an electrical engineer. It is not just enough for me to say "light can be a particle or a wave," nor do I just say, "we use a transmitter and a receiver in telecommunication." I cannot just tell people electromagnetic waves are used to transfer information and the process is called modulation and demodulation. I need to understand those guiding principles; therefore, I require to master the fundamentals. When the rudiments are mastered, building on it becomes an easier task, where you gain speed and stability.

And so, one way to learn rapidly is to focus on the fundamentals. If you miss the fundamentals, you have missed the substance. Once you miss the foundation, whatsoever you build on the faulty foundation will crumble. Many of us cannot appreciate what we are learning. We experience sudden burden and suffer brain compression because we missed the essentials.

A lot of Android programmers today who had fundamental skills in Java are finding it much easier than those who just came into this mobile app development age and wanted to start developing programs on Android studio. A lot of those who understand opening and closing tags in HTML and div tags in CSS are finding it easier working on web development today because they had the rudiments. This also implies that they will be ahead in learning rate than those who are just coming into the game. No matter how much you are eager to learn, you must dedicate some time to learning the fundamentals.

Remember the 20/80 rule states that 80% of what you accomplish is tied to 20% of certain actions. This 20% is from understanding the basics. In order to learn the things you desire to learn at a faster pace, spend more of your time understanding the nitty-gritty.

Even if you are learning tailoring, fashion designing, digital marketing or any other skill, the same rule applies.

You may have come across this advice before in other books. It is a reminder that this cannot be jettisoned.

Recently, I got a call from a lady who was running a network marketing business. She paid a lot of money to learn how to promote her goods and services using popular digital marketing platforms like Facebook and Instagram. But, what bothered her the most, was the fact that she paid a lot to learn these principles, but could not understand anything she was being taught. It made her feel so bad and she felt she wasn't as good as her other colleagues. She complained that she could not get value for the money she spent trying to learn digital marketing and because of the format at which the training was being conducted, there was a limit to how she could interact with her tutors.

So someone referred her to me, with the belief that I could help her. When I interviewed her, I asked her what exactly her problem was and she kept on saying she could not understand anything being taught in the class.

I asked what exactly her objective was?

She said her objective was to learn how to promote her network marketing beauty and cosmetic products using a popular digital marketing platform.

I replied casually that this is just using Facebook to promote your business nothing more and she said "yes" but that is what she does not know how to achieve.

I asked her, "do you know how to upload pictures and tag people on Facebook?" She said, "not really." I asked, "do you have a Facebook page?" Her reply was, "yes, I have a Facebook page and my Facebook page has 1000 friends." I said, "I am not asking if you have a Facebook profile. What I want to know is, do you have a Facebook page?" She said "well, I do not think I understand what you mean by 'Facebook page'." I asked, "what things were you taught during the lesson?" She said, "we were taught how to use tools like canvas and how to make videos for YouTube, how to use Facebook pixels and some advanced things; how to get followers and monetize their page." I asked "were you taught how to create a Facebook page?" She said, "they might have mentioned something like that but I am not sure." I realized that the challenge she had was that she had no fundamental skills and knowledge. She did not even understand how social networking works. She did not know the difference between a Facebook profile, Facebook page and Facebook group. She did not even know that Facebook can be linked with Instagram. While she had not committed any offense by not knowing these things, the very fact that she missed those aspects was a huge obstacle on her path to effective comprehension. Without the fundamentals, you can get lost in information transit. This simply implies that learning is not about the quantity of information you have, but how well you understand it.

This story says a lot as to why many are slow in learning.

This will make us appreciate that without understanding the very core principle supporting an idea, there is no way one can build successfully on that idea.

Let us talk about electromagnetism. Why are electromagnetic fields able to carry signals? It is through the process of modulation and demodulation. I spent a lot of years learning the terms modulation and demodulation, but I never understood exactly what they meant because typically in the electrical engineering syllabus, you hear a lot of concepts that you cannot wrap your head around. For example, you come across signal envelope, career frequency, modulating signals, fundamental frequency and you wonder what all these mean. And for someone who does not even understand the whole concept of electromagnetic waves, its application will become mind boggling.

At the fundamental, it simply means whenever you have an electric wave you have a magnetic wave, but both waves are out of phase with each other. Changing an electric wave creates a magnetic wave, and changing a magnetic wave creates an electric wave. Electromagnetic waves possess the three properties of analog signals which are frequency, amplitude, and phase. You cannot talk about frequency and of course amplitude if you are not referring to energy. Remember, according to Einstein's equation, there is a strong relationship between energy, mass, and speed and this relationship makes you understand that electromagnetic waves can move. They have motion, they can be propagated, they can be transmitted, they can be pushed; hence, just like a motor vehicle, they can be used to transmit information. Once these fundamentals are known, every other thing starts to build on it and then learning and comprehension is getting much easier, enjoyable and faster. My dear late lawyer friend used to explain the difference between murder and manslaughter. He used the basic principle of malice and so, I did not really need a law degree to be able to differentiate at this lower level the difference between the two. Nor did I have a hard time differentiating between a civil case and a criminal case.

I took lots of courses in business and marketing at one time in my life. Even though I was an engineering student, via the same principle of what we see daily around us, I was able to differentiate between "selling and marketing." I understood that marketing is value campaign while selling is where transactions occur.

If you want to be a programmer, depending on the language you are focused on, you need to first understand the basics of object-oriented programming.

What is an object? An object has a property.

Object-oriented programming is built around several concepts. These concepts are implemented using classes, objects, and methods, but it is useful to review those concepts more generally.

After that, you have the foundation to easily understand the Four core concepts of object-oriented programming which are abstraction, encapsulation, inheritance, and polymorphism.

IDENTIFY THE KEY FACTOR.

Learning swiftly does not mean focusing on just gaining time but competence. The essence of learning is to be equipped with sufficient knowledge to to offer solutions to a problem.

This also means that in your quest to expedite your learning, you should not derail from the KEY FACTORS.

For example, if you want to learn to drive.

The key factor is safety.

If you want to learn to cook.

The key factor is hygiene.

If you want to learn how to speak a new language.

The key factor is communication.

If you want to learn music production.

The key factor is making music that suits the purpose.

If you want to be a successful graduate

The key factor is good grades.

I learned as an undergraduate and while being an academic that the best students are necessarily not the ones with the best grades. A student of mine was able to explain black hole but when it came to documentation, he was poor at writing and it affected his grades. Upon seeing his past transcript and seeing that it wasn't a reflection of the student I knew, I sat him down and explained that, while I recognized that he was very smart, he should be aware that successful examination evaluation is pertinent to his scholarship.

I told him, "we do not grade what is in your head; we grade what you put on paper." So, a key factor to being a successful graduate lies in both good comprehension and good expression.

However, expression should not only be based on paperwork;

students can give expression in various other ways.

Trying to pay attention to the key factor may give you a slow start

but it will give you a strong footing and steady learning

experience.

Knowing why you are doing a thing contributes to knowing how.

SHOW ME

Moving over to our second point is to learn by illustration. It is not our fault that we need to excavate this classical way of learning and as the saying goes "you cannot change a winning team." Hence, one should not change a method that is working. It does not matter if we are in the 21st century or the 28th century, some learning aids help expedite the acquisition of knowledge.

You can doubt what you hear but not what you see.

This should be highlighted because lots of people search google but do not know what exactly to look for. It is your responsibility to know what to look for. The clue here is to focus on illustrative content.

Back to my illustration on the principle of modulation. A lot of students pretend they understand it, while they do not. Nobody wants to be left behind; still, nobody wants to be a dummy or perceived as one. Even though I strongly encourage people to always ensure that when being taught in the classroom, they seek clarity for whatever they do not understand, I also know from experience, that sometimes, even the size of the classroom or the emotional state of students you are teaching can hinder the way student wants to get involved in class. So, I encourage interaction which is one of the best ways to learn.

However, even while encouraging interaction, some students will just not participate. This requires a good lecturer who ensures that he/she does everything possible to pass knowledge at a faster rate and help his/her his students to develop quick understanding.

This reminds me of fast food.

Fast food is a type of mass-produced food designed for commercial resale with a strong priority placed on "speed of service" versus other relevant factors involved in culinary science. My dad used to tell me that fast food is food that is already prepared and ready for consumption with little preparation.

This is how illustrations make learning quicker and fun. A good teacher will refer to teaching aids to accelerate learning. Even learning languages can also adapt illustrative teaching aid to ensure the speed of learning and aid the memory. Quick learning has a lot to do with retentiveness.

During the coronavirus pandemic, a lot of audiovisual training lessons were being released. This is because it has been shown that people learn faster and they understand quicker when they learn with an illustration. The challenge however is that not everybody has the expertise to create interactivity, but this must strongly be encouraged. My recommendation is that teaching aids should be produced at every level, especially for technical courses using models, simulations, environments and other tools.

This will go a long way in helping students understand better. And for solo learners, ensure you look for resources that create illustrations.

There is no magic in our involvement in learning. No one, for now, can open the brain and pump bytes of information inside. Elon Musk plans to stream music directly into the brain. This can work well for music but for knowledge, we must participate in improving and adding to what we know.

Some time ago, a student of mine asked me, "Sir, can you kindly explain in layman's language the meaning of modulation?" I drew this object to illustrate it to him, and in less than 30 seconds what took me 5 years to understand was unraveled.

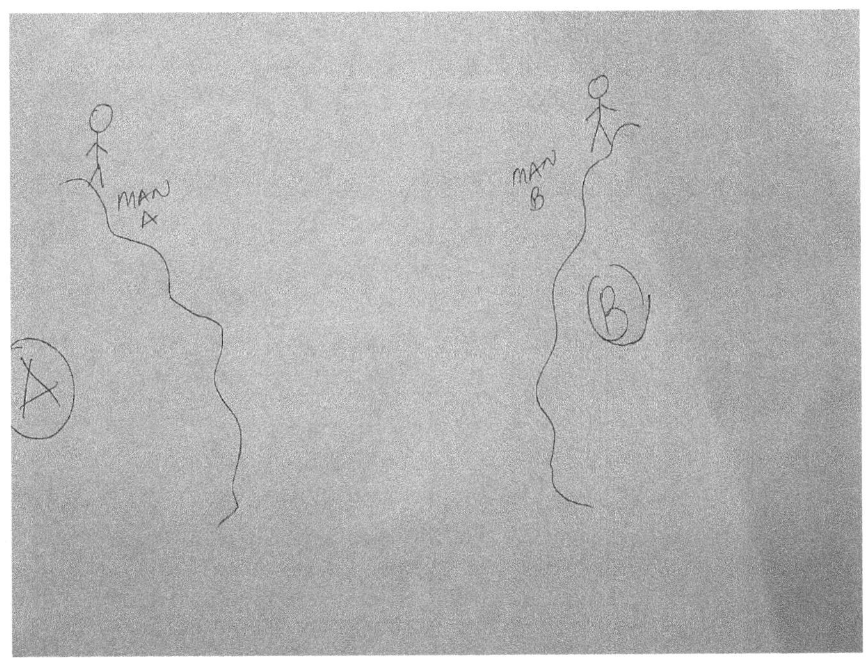

When you look at this image, Man A is trying to throw a paper to Man B, this is what we do in transmission; when we want to send the message from one point to another point. Now, looking at the diagram, you will observe that due to the presence of air resistance, gravity, lack of mass and wind, the paper cannot travel from point A to point B without missing its trajectory. This is what we simply call a channel in engineering. Channels can attenuate, impede, block, corrupt or ultimately even stop a signal from moving. Therefore, there should be a mechanism between point A and point B that can enable information to travel successfully. So all that Man A needs to do is to wrap the paper inside a stone and throw it to Man B. The stone helps the message to travel faster, and also helps to overcome the channel impairments because the weight of the stone generates momentum which can overcome gravity for the travel-time between the cliff, and when the paper gets to point B, all Man B needs to do is to unwrap the paper and retrieve the message. This was all I needed to explain the concept of modulation and demodulation. Many hours have been gained via this illustration.

I have used these methods to teach on principles of the microwave oven, heating elements, artificial neural networks for AI and lots of other engineering terms and it worked just well. No matter what you want to learn, always go for illustrations and visual aids. This will help you a lot.

PROJECT-ORIENTED LEARNING

This is remarkably like reverse engineering, where you dismantle an object, or you dismantle a piece of equipment to learn and see how it was fabricated

---

Next is what I call is "project-oriented learning." Let us assume you want to learn android studio. You can choose to first sit down and start with the end in mind. If you plan to build an eBook on the android app, target your learning and focus on learning tools and materials tools that specifically address how to build an eBook.

Recently, I was told to teach a particular subject and this subject had a lot of theoretical and practical aspects. For the sake of a structured curriculum, I wanted to ensure that I taught the whole theory and then the whole practical but I wanted to accelerate the rate at which my students learn. Therefore, I said to my students, "you guys are going to learn on the job." In this case, the workplace is the school. So I said, "this is how you are going to learn. Each of you will form a group of 5 students and I will give you a project so that at the end of every lecture, you will apply what I have taught you in realizing a prototype."

I came to realize that employing the advantage of learning by having a project will help you to remove redundancies. Usually, what Group A might need, group B might not need it. While the essence of going through a structured curriculum helps all groups to acquire the fundaments, when it comes to applying what they learn to build a project, we can easily establish that everything being taught in the class will automatically find expression when they are using it in real-time to build or construct something. This also can mean that learning a particular principle in social sciences or arts can be used to immediately write an article or a blog. This will help to learn rapidly. Through this process, the students will automatically pay attention to what they need from everything being taught to realize their project. This is similar to reverse engineering, where you dismantle an object, or you dismantle a piece of equipment to learn and see how it was fabricated. Inevitably, you will still have to consult the theory of the principles, but in this case, because you already have a prototype, by studying a working model you have skipped lots of hours of learning.

Let us study a principle used in speeding up the performance of microprocessors. I am going to talk about two important principles by which the speed of microprocessors increases. So the concept of learning on the job is targeted learning…

There was a time I wanted to learn python programming. Python has lots of applications and so I asked myself

"What exactly do I want to learn python for?"

I told myself," It's for Data science and AI."

Data science and AI is wide. I had to streamline it and I said, "I want to learn how to predict stock prize."

And so I started collecting all the libraries I needed.

Numpy, matplotlib, pandas etc and that was it. And at the end, I did not only learn that application; I had a faster grip on using python for a whole lot of applications too.

MY-COPROCESSOR

The quest for speed is what separated a revolution from another.

The 4th industrial revolution is built on speed

Everything changed when man started looking for speed. The quest for speed is what separated a revolution from another. The 4th industrial revolution is built on speed. Let us study briefly two ways the microprocessor increased its speed over the years.

CACHE

In a cache, frequently used instructions are kept in a special dedicated memory location because the processor is aware that these instructions are used more often than others. Let me use a simple illustration. During the coronavirus pandemic, the sales of hydroxychloroquine surged, and every pharmacy needed to stock up hydroxychloroquine because of the frequent order. But by intuition, what is the essence of keeping the drugs hidden when you know that due to the current situation in the world, you can easily predict that a large percentage of your buyers will request to buy hydroxychloroquine or any flu-related medication? Hence, those are the items you will want to keep on your front desk making it is easier for you or the sales personnel to easily reach out for this product when it is in demand. This is the same principle of cache memory in microprocessors. This has gone a long way in helping microprocessors to increase in speed. And can also help you to learn speedily. By learning with a project you are working on, you will only use what you need and will leave other unused tools for later.

It goes on to say if you want to learn how to weld or want to learn how to build an e-Commerce website with PHP/MYSQL or an e-Commerce Android application, you start consulting those things that are important and necessary. Probably you will start coming across some already developed plugins and all you need to do is to put these tools together and use your Java code or

PHP or HTML to tie them up together. By so doing, you have compressed many years, sessions, and periods of learning into one single easy piece of a project. This is highly effective. The spinoff is that while working on that project and you completed it successfully, it will help you when you come across other similar projects. You just need to make some modifications and you will be right on track with the new project. If you want to learn how to bake, start with your project. For example, a chocolate cake. Here you will learn the general principles of baking; how to mix the cake, how to measure the sugar. Those skills come in the process but at the end of the day, you have not only known how to bake a cake; you now know how to make a chocolate cake. Two things learned in a single session, because you learned on the job, and you started learning from it, and in that process, because there are some ingredients almost uniform to all cake processes, you will also have opportunity to master the fundamentals.

Usually, in many applications, there are templates. These templates are not installed just to show the features or capabilities of these applications, but to also allow you to learn how to use them faster. Not everyone is aware of these templates. Hence, it makes learning slower.

There is a caveat though. If you want to learn how to drive a car, do not start by driving yourself to a nearby village. In this case, you take time to learn the rudiments, and then you pick on from there.

HYPERTHREADING

Another principle processors use in accelerating speed and performances is Hyper-threading. Hyper-threading (officially called Hyper-Threading Technology or HT Technology and abbreviated as HTT or HT) is Intel's proprietary simultaneous multithreading (SMT) implementation used to improve parallelization of computations (doing multiple tasks at once) performed on x86 microprocessors.

If you want to learn a language, start by writing a storybook in that language. You will go through a lot of initial hardship, but by the time you have written 5 pages, you will realize how much you have learned in such a short time.

Hyper-threading is another principle used to increase the speed of microprocessors. It is simply the parallel computation, that is like multitasking. Somebody might ask that if I multitask, will I be an effective learner? if you learn to multitask, you will learn more rapidly. Am I saying the brain can do two things at the same time? I am using multitasking here to illustrate that you can learn and apply what you lean simultaneously and while learning, you can divide the process into two that runs not literally concurrently but runs concurrently in the principle of learn-and-do. So, if somebody is trying to teach you how to build a sculpture, it tells you what you need to do and then you do it. Therefore, you are learning by direct instruction and practice; as you are being instructed, you apply the principles you are being taught. This can enable you to learn much faster than you would if you had no project on the ground.

There is no shortcut; these are the options available to accelerate learning.

Once, a friend of mine wanted to go into large scale ginger farming and during an inspection of the farm, an expert assumed and told my friend that the possibility of the farm being successful is very low, because according to the expert, my friend did not consult with other experts before engaging in the process. While it is particularly important to always carry the expert along, and my friend carried some experts along, something that was inevitable was that my friend gained a lot of knowledge from his experience. He learned where he had to improve, what he had to stop, what he had to continue and in a short time he learned swifter about what it meant to farm ginger successfully. This was his first time. He learned on the job. And in short time he became a consultant.

During the coronavirus pandemic, Bill Gates, a computer software developer, took the center stage in the discussion of a pandemic control and vaccine, even more than some medical practitioners, because by interacting with societies and getting involved in programs which had dealt with past viruses like Ebola, Lassa fever, SARS, Polio, swine flu, etc., Bill Gates accelerated his learning and understanding of how viruses and vaccine work. This does not make him a licensed doctor. We are not talking about how to be licensed personnel, but how to learn faster and contribute to society by finding solutions to problems. So today, whenever viruses are being discussed, Bill Gates is consulted, not due to his financial contribution, but because of the skills and competence he has demonstrated when discussing the issue of viruses and vaccines.

COMPETITIVE LEARNING

One of the reasons why people do not learn faster is because

there is a problem with their motivation

One of the reasons why people do not learn faster is because there is a problem with their motivation. I call it a trigger. If you have a deadline to meet, if you have an incentive If you have a prize waiting for you, this will motivate you to be a rapid learner. Competitive learning is a principle we use in artificial intelligence. Competitive learning is a form of unsupervised learning in artificial neural networks, in which nodes compete for the right to respond to a subset of the input data. Models and algorithms based on the principle of competitive learning include vector quantization and self-organizing

Competitive learning principles are used in artificial intelligence where different terminals contend for the right to respond to a subset of imputed data. Perhaps our society is behind in learning because we have not engaged in any form of competitive learning. The incentives are low and the high paying jobs to encourage learning are not available. BUT with the advent of remote jobs, some jobs pay as high as $93,000. And the best of the best is targeting this high prize. If you want to learn, you need to learn competitively. This can be done either by learning for a price. Also, you should give yourself a target; this gives more motivation as well. **Competitive learning helps your mind to be energetic; to be alert and alive and it helps you to accelerate the rate of learning.**

I remember when I started learning Artificial intelligence,

A friend needed to build an AI system for voltage stabilization.

The stability must be intelligently compensated.

When he told me - even though I was an engineer - I did not know JACK about what to do. So I told him I will ask a friend in South Africa to do it for him.

That night I opened an Artificial neural network tutorial on YouTube.

I bought a data bundle for internet access,

I called a friend for consultation.

I prayed for inspiration and guidance.

I started reading and started putting one and one together.

I started studying the process of supervised and unsupervised learning.

I started studying what clustering, classification, regression etc. meant.

I started studying the meaning of training, validation, and test data.

It started making sense to me and at the end of the day, it was a distinction for my friend and a MAJOR leap in my career.

Many times, we ignore the fundamentals.

Once the fundamentals are understood,

A fundamental milestone has been achieved

Recall hyper-threading, in which computation is carried out in parallel microprocessors. Also use the principal of co-processing to accelerate the way by which they learn. Two is better than one is a divine principle. Because co-processors are designed to complete special functions, it helps the general speed of the micro processing units. Competitive lending helps you optimize your learning curve because it forces you to respond to an incentive.

TELL THE PUBLIC

Sometimes you need to set up yourself for public scrutiny

To accelerate learning,

Throw a challenge.

Yes, you need a trigger.

You need something to hold you accountable.

You need to put yourself in the spotlight.

You need to setup a surveillance program for your self

When you know people will hold you accountable, you will come

alive.

I have spoken to several people. What I discovered is that the

problem of motivation is a major issue why people do not learn fast. They lack the motivation and until this issue is addressed, they would keep on suffering from low and nonproductive learning. If you want to give yourself some much-needed motivation, you need to set up yourself for public scrutiny. **Sometimes you need to put yourself on the line; sometimes you need to set up a public challenge for yourself. You just need the right trigger to make your brain operation optimized.** For example, if you want to learn how to make a particular meal, tell people about it, Let them anticipate, let them wait, let them expect, and let them ask you for it. It will amaze you that your behavior will change, you will think better, act more proactively, you will not want to disappoint their expectations and you will expedite your learning process.

HOW TO KNOW WHAT YOU DO NOT KNOW

FIND A GROUP

As an undergraduate student. I had time to take some analysis of my performance at two different semesters. I realized that I performed better at semesters where I studied with a group of people than at semesters where I was a solo learner. Usually, the popularity of the "learn-at-home" system is not to encourage isolation learning but to encourage 'convenient learning,' Learning at home should NOT be confused with learning in isolation. Create a group, WhatsApp, Facebook and work together.

Learning in a group have lots of advantages. First, it is important to define what we mean by the group. A group in this context, is two people and above. So, we know that two is always better than one. We can appreciate the progress the world has made with the initiation of social media. This only comes to show that the social experiment of interconnecting people in a large network has really propagated the world positively in many directions. People who can form smaller groups and discuss issues of common interest have seen themselves emerge with more confidence in the subject matter. It is imperative in some instances that coming together as a group to discuss and to learn is almost inevitable. For example, in politics and issues around health and society. The major motivation why people come in groups is because so many perspectives are presented, and everyone standing at a different position is able to see things differently and also offer diverse opinion, which if considered objectively, can be used to advance a cause or a profitable progressive idea. Therefore, we can also take from this system to accelerate how we learn by forming a cluster or looking for societies which are interested or are also pursuing the same objectives as we are pursuing. During interaction, one of the first things you will notice is that not everyone knows the same thing at the same time. This will emulate the parallel computation of microprocessors that we spoke about earlier. **You will realize that through this interactive forum, you will not only learn, you will also discover what you do not know and this is why it is very important to ask questions.**

CROSS-EXAMINATION

Often there are many things you know already. Accelerating your learning begins from being able to filter between what you know and what you do not know. Therefore, a teacher is encouraged to always allow students to ask questions. Because that is how insight is gained into the 20% of the 80% that will speed up the student assimilating.

Why do lawyers cross examine their witnesses? Because through cross-examination you are not only able to gather facts, you are able to create relationship between facts. The whole essence of accelerated learning is your ability to readily connect different nodes of knowledge into a major piece that you can apply and use to solve your problems. The advantage here is that many of the nodes do not originate from you. By virtue of your group association, many parallel contributions come from different angles that now forms into your mind and becomes your intellectual property. So being in a group, even if it is a group of two people in principle ensures that you are able to increase the rate at which you learn compared to if you were alone.

GET INVOLVED IN TEACHING IT

Many years ago, as young boy of 12, I discovered that when I talk to my invisible audience alone in my room, I tend to remember more and understand faster. This I later realized was also promoted as Feynman Technique.

Talk about it...Teach it...this strategy works like magic...one way to learn is to teach it.

There are many things I wanted to learn that I started learning when I was teaching them. It sounds funny and ironically, but it works.

This is part of a reward system and a trigger that serves as incentives which motivate and improve brain activities.

Human responds to rewards.

Humans needs drive.

Humans needs a push.

This is a fantasy story that illustrates an important principle of life. It was a man trying to walk across a cliff. There was a short ladder. The ladder was just at the tip of where his legs where. He asked a man standing by," how do you expect me to walk to the other end of the Cliff without a ladder?" The man replied him, "sometimes you never find your way until you step out on the journey. Put your leg on the ladder and you will see what I mean." So as the man put his one leg on the first rung of the ladder, another rung of the ladder appeared and as he put his other leg, another rung of the ladder appeared, and as he kept walking, the ladder became longer and longer and longer till he got to the end of the cliff.

One of the best ways to learn is to teach what you want to learn. This serves as an incentive and the motivation for you. As soon as you know someone or people are depending on you to learn this will fast-track your learning process. It does not have to be an official appointment or a paid appointment. You may just choose to set up this system in order for you to get the right reward for learning. I assure you from experience this method works well.

The neurons in the human brain are programmed to be activated. Electric pulses have a way of triggering our neural structure and this can have a reaction all over the human body. When the brain is challenged, it tends to automatically adjust for optimal performance. Even when you look at the small mouse trying to escape from danger. It is able to consider multiple actions at once because the brain activity has been increased dramatically. We human beings can also benefit from such accelerated enthusiasm, improving our learning rates. This can be one of such triggers that can throw the brain into a state of optimized performance.

LEARNING FOR INNOVATION THROUGH IMITATION

Imitation is a powerful principle that you can employ in being

creative.

Take ideas from what people have done and see how you can

improve on them. That is part of creative thinking. Imitation to

innovation. This can help you learn with the speed of a cheetah.

Taking the first step is the most important and I always call the

first step the giant step no matter how small or tiny it is.

The first step is the seed step, and it is the investment step. It is

the conception step, and it is the step that starts the process to a

long and lasting journey

One major challenge we usually encounter when at the embryonic stage of an idea or concept is knowing what to do. For example, imagine if you want to develop a business plan or you want to design a house or you want to build a prototype or want to start an e-commerce business.

That period you wake up and sit in front of your PC is a particularly important area in the life cycle of your dreams. Because if you miss that opportunity, you may relapse into another period of procrastination and coma.

So, let me tell you what to do.

Always start with an imitation.

Do not task your brain or force it to want to puke out new ideas or concepts.

Do not force your brain till it is unwilling to cooperate with you.

Make it easy for the brain by starting with a sample that you can initiate and copy and then from imitation, you move over to innovation.

Imitation is a powerful principle that you can employ in being creative.

Many phenomenal ideas you see today were innovation on what was existing somewhere before.

There is NOTHING NEW under the sun

Often I'm always surprised when I discuss with research students who seem to have a lot of problems understanding a particular principle or concept and when I ask them, "this thing you are trying to do, have you consulted someone who has done it before?" Sometimes they will say, "no" and sometimes they're not so sure of my question. And I always used to tell them, one of the easiest ways to accelerate what you are learning, is you need to learn how to imitate. So, this is a principle that is being used by the most successful apprenticeship system in the world and even in Nigeria. Somebody says, "If I had my way, I will go to a role model. I will go to a mentor. I would ask to work for my mentor for three months without pay" because what you will learn by observation, what you will learn by imitation you might not learn it on your own no matter how many books or videos you watch. So when an apprentice is working with a man who is involved in a particular business, all he needs to do is to observe and to imitate. Observation and imitation are enormously powerful principles that you can use to learn. If somebody marketed a particular product effectively, all you need to do is to copy his method and acknowledge it when due. You do not have to start from scratch. Of course, based on the uniqueness of what you are marketing, it will be natural for you to introduce some changes, some tweaks, amendments and some alterations along the way, but fundamentally, you will realize that you have been able to compress hours and hours and days and days and months and months of research just by imitating and following what someone has already done and achieved. This is one of the ways to increase and to learn. If you want to build a website, if you want to learn how to build a mobile app, if you want to learn and understand a particular principle in mathematics, even if you want to learn how to speak in an English test, all you need to do is to look at someone who has done it well, and imitate learning.

The Asians utilized this principle to accelerate their industrialization process.

To imitate is not a weakness. It is a strategy that helps you to deal with redundancy; that helps you to jettison a waste of time and also helps you to fast-track your learning. Imitation is enormously powerful. It is very important and is very necessary if you must learn quicker.

CONTACT TRACING

You need to make the sacrifice of engaging experts in the field of what you want to learn

A guy came up with a brilliant idea of inviting authors to his studio and made them give abridged versions of their books. Undoubtedly, this is going to help people to learn whatsoever is written in that book faster because having contact with the author is having contact with the source of the information in the book. Therefore, it is your responsibility to establish effective "contact tracing" either by finding how to contact the author which is not easy or probable or by looking for anyone who has had contact with a particular competence and skill you are trying to learn.

Note, in this case you are not just looking for teachers or trainers, you are looking for a coach and a mentor. You need to take the sacrifice of engaging experts in the field of what you want to learn. Someone might say "but this is basic and everyone knows this." Yes! I do not have any doubts that engaging specialists in a particular field will help you to learn faster but the difficulty in identifying who to locate in order to learn these things is not as easy as expected. That is why I call it "contact tracing." How do you perform this type of contact tracing? You need to actively join societies, social media groups communities. This is an extension of looking for a group to learn but in this case you are looking to establish a more personal type of oriented relationship with someone you have identified may have made contact with a source of knowledge.

There was a time I wanted to learn how to publish a book. I went through some social media comments and I was able to locate someone who I knew had knowledge about book publishing on that platform. I contacted him and we setup an appointment.

And in no time, I developed proficiency in doing that.

TIPS TO KNOW PEOPLE FASTER

Do you know it is particularly important also to learn about people faster?

People are assets but also some can be a liability to you. Relating or working with the right people can mean lots of success for you, and the wrong people can be losses as well.

I can tell you from experience that I lacked this skill at a time in my life and it was a costly prize I paid. **You need to learn this ability of studying people and gaining some rapid insight into their personality.** Because you may be required by virtue of a new environment and opportunity to meet different sorts of people. And you do not have the time to spend with them before you form your opinion them. Making one wrong or right move can break or make you.

As I mentioned earlier, there was a time I was not fast or keen enough to study the character of some persons and it was an exceedingly high price for me. But today I know better. And I attempt to gain insight into people personality before I engage in any crucial dealing with them.

Of course, you cannot know everything about a person at a go. But you don not always have the luxury of time and missing this can be a matter of life and death for your career or business. It can even be consequential also in your life, relationship, and marriages.

Many people will not tell you about themselves on the platter of gold, not because they do not want to, but because they too, even though they might think but yet do not know who they.

They might end up telling you who they think they are, or who they wish or hope they are. They can create an impression of what they genuinely what to be, but you must be careful about building a decision around an impression.

Someone tells you he/she is hardworking. That might be a wish. Therefore, you must create your own algorithms for learning about people faster. How do you know someone is honest? how do you know is reliable? how do you know someone is religious? and how do you know someone is smart? How do you know pretense from reality?

One key I will like to give to you is observation. If you want to learn about someone faster, you might not have to cross-examine the person or engage in a torrent of questions. This will not even be feasible when dealing with people. But you need to observe they behave around others. Do not build your judgment based on how they behave around you but based on how they behave around others. This is particularly important. If someone tells you he/she is honest to you, but you observe dishonesty to other people, that is what you should believe by default. I remember some years ago, someone once told me how he manipulated a system for his own personal advantage. I was foolish enough to think he will not do the same thing to me. I was obviously wrong because this person's character was unchangeable. All I needed to have known is that principle that says. If someone shows you who they are believe them. Once, a young man who has a lot of interest in making me comfortable whenever am around him, sat with me for three hours telling me his ordeals in life and how he was always accused of theft even while he's innocent. He gave lots of instances in the past when he was being accused of stealing and later exonerated. At That point, I was more concerned about his accusers and not him and I discussed with one of his accusers who told me a totally different side of the story. I was still at the verge of making my judgement about him, when two days after that in a separate incidence, he confessed to stealing some sensitive materials and was arrested.

So, observe how to behave and others. This also goes to say observe how they are in a group. When you meet someone with exceptionally good team behavior that can tell you a lot about the person's values.

People are usually not what they do to you, they are what they do to others. So, do not ever conclude based on how they behave with you but on how they behave with others. In so doing, you have not created a three-dimensional object with greater details and greater perspectives. Two other things to study in people are their natural response to crises and their biases. This will be discussed later.

WHAT IS YOUR SKILL INVENTORY?

92

We are in the era of skills; many people are taking personal responsibility to ensure they meet up the demands of a technologically advancing world.

We are in the era of skills; many people are taking personal responsibility to ensure they meet up to the demands of a technologically advancing world.

Of a truth, education is key to success not because of a certificate but because true education equips you with competency and know-how to become a solution provider, an entrepreneur and an intra-prenuer.

Recently I was interviewed by an author who was gathering facts for his new book and he asked me a lot of questions. He asked me if there was something I wished I knew some years ago and I recalled Mark Zuckerberg's comment that the "best way to predict the future is to invent it." I told him that years ago we were rightly encouraged to get the best grades. A piece of advice I still recommend today, BUT we weren't taught to get the best skills.

Skills is the future of the labor market because the world of tomorrow will be solution-driven.

People will need better ways of doing things, better ways of delivering services, better ways of farming and food security, better ways of entertainment and media, better ways of video compression and cloud optimization, better ways of politics and campaign, better ways of delivering religious content and books, better ways of marketing and selling, better ways of teaching and learning, better ways of e-health and mental wellbeing. What I usually tell people is the more advanced technology goes the easier things becomes.

One psychological drag many have is they feel the world has moved in such a hurry, hence they can't catch up. This is not true.

There is still time to be an expert…

All you need is to have a passion and a learning plan.

Give yourself 1 year to master an act.

There are more schools online now that have ever been,

The earlier the better.

We need to START TODAY and START somewhere.

The greatest regret will be for those who had the opportunity in 2020 to become experts but conceded to the struggle and distraction of daily life.

There is still time to become an expert.

A PEEK INTO THE NEXT PHASE OF THIS BOOK

The world is preparing for a massive revolution and change in the way we do things such as has never been seen before

---

Skills in demand is largely dependent on the direction a society wants to head to. Many developed countries have had to provide lots of incentives, even path to citizenship in exchange for sourcing of skilled workers into their system to mount and power various parts pertinent to their economy. While some other countries look inwards to build manpower and skills to power their own economic ecosystem.

The world is preparing for a massive revolution and change in the way we do things such as has never been seen before.

Remember the stone age did not end because there were no more stones; rather because men started thinking ahead.

The richest man today as at the time of writing this book is Jeff Bezos. Amazon is an e-commerce and service driven industry and the wealth accrued because of innovation and tools that brought about a new way of doing things.

Software development	Artificial intelligence	Digital marketing	Agriculture
Web/ Mobile technology	Data science	Cryptocurrency and blockchain	e-commerce
Health delivery and vaccine	Remote learning	Fashion	Robotics and Automation
Renewable energy	Autonomous vehicle	Public speaking	Logistics
Entertainment	Graphics	Media	Critical thinking

Human basic needs barely change. Essentials will always be essentials. Using the Maslow hierarchy of human needs, talking about food, health, clothes, shelter, mental health, entertainment beauty. These will always be the needs of and wants of people.

What will change however, is access to these things. This is where there will be massive solutions and products and the way things are done will be forever changed. This is just the beginning of a new chapter...

Oluseun D Oyeleke is a Bachelor and master's degree holder in Electrical /Electronics and Communications Engineering. He is currently a PhD research student with interest in microwave and machine learning applications.

He is a Lecturer, Author, motivational speaker, entrepreneur, and a student.

He is the founder of The Greatlight visionaries and online community of leaders and Edutronic hub. He has been teaching and mentoring young people for the past 20 years.

He has a passion for Education, and he is the Program Director of the READ project. He wants to inspire young leaders all over Africa.

Oluseun is married to his namesake Oluwaseun Tinuade, an entrepreneur and they have a son. Together they are working to pursue their vision and passion of inspiring success and building leaders.

Oluseun Oyeleke wikiman

http://oluseunwikiman.com/

https://www.facebook.com/Greatlightt

https://twitter.com/Oluseunwikiman

iamwikiman

 +2348036546874

TO INVITE THE AUTHOR FOR PUBLIC

SPEAKING,CONSULTING,TRAINING AND OTHER EVENTS

CALL +2348036546874 or email contactseun@gmail.com

VISIT

http://oluseunwikiman.com/

www.ingramcontent.com/pod-product-compliance
Lightning Source LLC
Chambersburg PA
CBHW071927120726
48001CB00005B/1905